Simple Machines in the Great Outdoors

Gillian Gosman

PowerKiDS press

New York

For Roger and George

Published in 2015 by The Rosen Publishing Group, Inc.
29 East 21st Street, New York, NY 10010

First Edition

Book Design: Joe Carney
Photo Research: Katie Stryker

Photo Credits: Cover InavanHateren/Shutterstock.com; p. 4 Piotr Wawrzyniuk/Shutterstock.com; p. 5 destillat/iStock/Thinkstock; p. 6 Steve Estvanik/Shutterstock.com; p. 7 Taylor S. Kennedy/National Geographic/Getty Images; p. 8 Andrey Plis/Shutterstock.com; p. 9 aragami12345s/Shutterstock.com; p. 10 EpicStockMedia/Shutterstock.com; p. 11 Nicram Sabod/Shutterstock.com; p. 12 iofoto/Shutterstock.com; p. 13 Pierdelune/Shutterstock.com; p. 14 Lost Horizon Images/Cultura/Getty Images; p. 15 Adie Bush/Cultura/Getty Images; p. 16 Maxim Petrichuk/Shutterstock.com; p. 17 manit321/Shutterstock.com; p. 18 Vishnevskiy Vasily/Shutterstock.com; p. 19 My Good Images/Shutterstock.com; p. 20 Paolo_Toffanin/iStock/Thinkstock; p. 21 oliveromg/Shutterstock.com; p. 22 Goodluz/Shutterstock.com.

Library of Congress Cataloging-in-Publication Data

Gosman, Gillian, author.
 Simple machines in the great outdoors / by Gillian Gosman. — First edition.
    pages cm. — (Simple machines everywhere)
 Includes index.
 ISBN 978-1-4777-6837-2 (library binding) — ISBN 978-1-4777-6838-9 (pbk.) — ISBN 978-1-4777-6642-2 (6-pack)
 1. Simple machines—Juvenile literature. 2. Machinery—Juvenile literature. 3. Outdoor recreation—Juvenile literature. I. Title.
 TJ147.G684 2015
 621.8—dc23
                                    2013048490

Manufactured in the United States of America

CPSIA Compliance Information: Batch #WS14PK5: For Further Information contact Rosen Publishing, New York, New York at 1-800-237-9932

Contents

What Are Simple Machines?

In your home, at school, and on the road, simple machines are put to work. They are tools that people use to multiply or redirect the **force** we put toward a task. There are six different simple machines. They are the inclined plane, the wedge, the screw, the lever, the pulley, and the wheel and axle.

These girls are using several simple machines. The bow, or front, of the kayak is a wedge. The kayak paddle is a lever.

Simple machines help get us to our outdoor destinations! Here you can see ski lifts moving up and down a mountain. The lifts are moved along using pulleys, a type of simple machine.

Simple machines help us enjoy the great outdoors. They help us camp, fish, play games, and much more. On land, at sea, or in the air, we love simple machines!

It's Plane to See

This hiking trail goes along the side of the mountain. It slowly slopes upward, making the hike a little easier.

An inclined plane is a **slope** with one raised end. Moving an object along a slope requires less **effort**, or force, than lifting or lowering the object the height of the plane.

Think about the winding hiking trails that go around a hill or mountain from the base to the summit, or highest point. These trails are inclined planes! The sloped paths allow hikers to go up or down the height of the hill or mountain with much less effort than it would take to climb straight up.

Some slopes are too steep to go straight up. In these cases, trails will often be zigzagged, making the climb less intense.

Wedges in Winter Weather

Mountain climbers use picks, like the one shown here, to help them climb. The pick is wedge shaped and can be driven into ice.

A wedge is a simple machine that can both drive objects apart and hold them together. We insert the narrow edge of the wedge into an object, and the wedge multiplies the effort and redirects our downward force to the sides.

Picture a mountain climber working her way across a sheet of icy snow. She wears boots with spiked soles and carries a pick in her hand. The boots' spikes and the ice pick are wedges that hold their place in the snow and ice to provide **traction** and **leverage** for the climber.

The spikes, or wedges, on the soles of these climbing boots help climbers get traction on slippery surfaces. When the climber steps, the spikes are driven into the ice.

A Special Screw

A screw is a rod with a twisting ridge, called a thread, around it. Many screws, such as wood screws, have pointed ends and flat ends. If you apply a twisting force to the flat head, the screw's thread lifts the material around it, drawing the screw into the object.

When camping in a harsh, windy climate, it is important to have a secure tent. Screwing the tent into the ground keeps it from slipping or being blown away.

This climber's rope is strung through two carabiners. Each carabiner's locking part has a screw inside it. You lock the carabiner by twisting this part up or down.

Whenever outdoor **equipment**, such as a shelter for ice fishing or an ice climber's tent, needs to be secured to ice or frozen ground, a screw is an excellent choice. Mountain climbers secure their harnesses and ropes with **carabiners** that screw into a locked position. Also, canteen lids screw closed.

The Likable Lever

A lever is any object that **pivots** on a fulcrum, or fixed point, to lift, push, or pull a load. Levers are divided into three classes based on where the fulcrum is in relation to the load and effort.

Fishing rods are third-class levers. You apply effort to them between the fulcrum and the load.

Wheelbarrows are very useful when you are doing garden work outdoors. They are also second-class levers.

Effort

Effort

Load

Fulcrum

Have you ever seen a hand pump at a campsite or park? These pumps use the power of a lever to draw water from deep underground to the surface. They are also first-class levers. You apply effort to the end of the handle. This is on the opposite side of the fulcrum from pump parts and water that make up the load.

Pulling Their Weight

Some pulleys are movable. Others are fixed. If you use a movable pulley along with a fixed pulley, you will need to apply less effort to move your load.

Load

Movable pulley

Effort

Fixed pulley

A pulley is a grooved wheel. A rope, chain, or cable is set in the groove. Applying effort to one end of the rope raises or lowers a load attached to the other end of the rope. Using pulleys in groups increases their mechanical advantage, or amount by which the force applied to them is multiplied.

Pulleys are very common on sailboats to raise, lower, loosen, or tighten the sails. Mountain climbers also use pulleys. The climber anchors the pulley at the top of the climb and attaches his harness to one end. A fellow mountain climber holds the other end.

Pulleys are very useful when rock climbing. They help climbers move up the rocks they are climbing. They also help them safely descend.

The Wondrous Wheel and Axle

When this mountain biker presses down on his pedals, the attached gears turn the axle on the back wheel of the bike. The axle turns the wheel.

A wheel and axle is made up of a large wheel fixed to a narrow rod called an axle. Effort is applied to the axle to make it turn. The wheel's **circumference** is larger, so its **rotation** covers more ground than the axle's rotation.

The wheel and axle is, of course, very important in wheeled vehicles, such as bicycles. It is also at the heart of countless other inventions, including waterwheels, windmills, and paddleboats. Mountain biking is a great way to use wheels and axles to see nature.

The rotation of a wheel can also be used to make an attached axle rotate. The axle's rotation covers less distance than the wheel's does, but the force with which it rotates is greater. This is how waterwheels work.

Water turns wheel

Wheel turns axle

Find Them in Nature

Humans have put the laws of **physics** to great use and created countless tools using the six simple machines. Simple machines also occur on their own in nature.

The great spotted woodpecker uses its wedge-shaped beak to peck into trees. It does this to find food and to build nests inside of trees.

In a sense, any hill is an inclined plane. Walking up a sloped hill is much easier than climbing a cliff! A bird's beak and a tiger's tooth are both powerful wedges for driving objects apart. Birds use their wedge-shaped beaks to dig into the ground and trees for food. Our own jointed arms work as levers, pivoting around the fulcrum of the elbow.

Our knees also act as fulcrums. Bending them as we walk, run, or climb helps us move more quickly with less effort. Try walking with your legs straight and see the difference knees make!

Now It Gets Complex

The narrow end of the wedge-shaped ax cuts into wood. Axes are used for many things, including chopping wood for fires.

Humans have been using simple machines since the earliest civilizations built, worked, and played. Over time, though, we have also created more complex machines. These **compound** machines are made up of two or more simple machines.

Wood axes have been used for thousands of years to cut down trees. Axes are compound machines. The cutting blade is a wedge, and the long handle is a lever, pivoting at the point where it is gripped by the user's hand. A garden hoe is another compound machine that uses a wedge and a lever. Zip lines depend on both inclined planes and pulleys.

All wheelbarrows are levers. The slope of this one's bucket adds an inclined plane, shifting the weight to where it is easiest to carry.

Thank You, Simple Machines!

The six simple machines we have explored in this book are everywhere. Look around you and thank the mechanical heroes in your midst!

Simple machines are especially helpful when we try to make our way in the great outdoors. Using the inclined plane, the wedge, the screw, the pulley, and the wheel and axle, people have invented countless technologies that allow us to tame, enjoy, and take advantage of all that the great outdoors has to offer.

Simple machines are all around us, helping us enjoy nature. Do you see the simple machine in this photograph?

Glossary

carabiners (ker-uh-BEE-nerz) Rings that hold and lock rope.

circumference (ser-KUMP-fernts) The distance around something circular.

compound (KOM-pownd) Two or more things combined.

effort (EH-fert) The amount of force applied to an object.

equipment (uh-KWIP-mint) All the supplies needed to do an activity.

force (FORS) Something that moves or pushes on something else.

leverage (LEH-veh-rij) The added help of using a machine to do work.

physics (FIH-ziks) The scientific study of matter and energy and their relationships to each other.

pivots (PIH-vuts) Turns on a fixed point.

rotation (roh-TAY-shun) The spinning motion of moving in a circle.

slope (SLOHP) A hill.

traction (TRAK-shun) The grip a moving object has on a surface.

Index

C

carabiners, 11
circumference, 16

E

effort, 4, 7–8,
    12–14, 16
equipment, 11

F

force, 4, 7, 8, 10, 14
fulcrum, 12–13, 19

I

inclined plane(s), 4, 7,
    19, 21, 22

L

leverage, 9
lever(s), 4, 12–13,
    19, 21

P

physics, 18
pulley(s), 4, 14–15, 22

S

screw, 4, 10–11, 22
slope, 7

T

tools, 4, 18

W

wedge(s), 4, 8–9, 19,
    21–22
wheel and axle(s),
    4, 16–17

Websites

Due to the changing nature of Internet links, PowerKids Press has developed an online list of websites related to the subject of this book. This site is updated regularly. Please use this link to access the list: www.powerkidslinks.com/sme/out/